時代英語

Fun *with*
Chinese Idioms

Ching Yee • John Smithback

FEDERAL PUBLICATIONS
Singapore • Kuala Lumpur • Hong Kong

ISBN 981 01 3070 8

Cover design by Ching Yee Smithback

Printed by South East Printing Pte Ltd, Singapore

爱 财 如 命
ài　　cái　　rú　　mìng

形容非常贪爱钱财。

他愈富有，愈爱财如命，不许别人分享他一分一毫。

爱 love　　财 wealth　　如 as　　命 life

To be obsessed with the possession and pursuit of wealth.
English equivalents: Be a money-grubber; A Scrooge.

百　折　不　挠
bǎi　zhé　bù　náo

意志坚强，屡受挫折但不屈服。

他屡次失败，仍然百折不挠，反而加倍练习，坚决在下届运动会夺得撑竿跳高冠军。

百 **hundred**	折 **setbacks**	不 **not**
挠 **deterred**		

Undeterred by many setbacks.
English equivalents: Fight to the bitter end; Never say die; Stick it out.

半 斤 八 两
bàn jīn bā liǎng

指两物的重量相等。也比喻彼此不分高下。

你聪明，他机警，斗智起来，大家半斤八两。

半 half   斤 catty   八 eight   两 taels

A catty, a unit of weight, equals 16 taels (approximately 21 ounces). This term initially referred to two things of equal weight; it now describes two people of equal stature or talent.
English equivalents: Six of one and a half dozen of the other; Tweedledum and tweedledee.

包 藏 祸 心
bāo　cáng　huò　xīn

暗中怀着害人的念头。

看他行为有点古怪，可能包藏祸心，我们要
小心提防。

包 contain　藏 hide　祸 sinister　心 heart

To harbour an evil intention.
English equivalents: A stab in the back; The
bait hides the hook.

本 末 倒 置

běn　　mò　　dào　　zhì

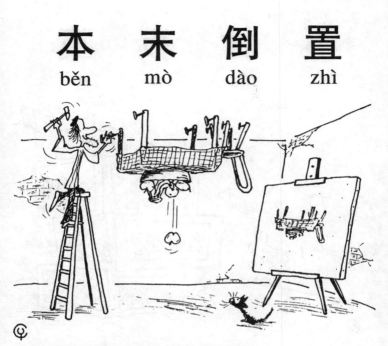

把事情的重点和细节颠倒处理。

他办事没有条理，常常本末倒置，弄到事情不可收拾。

本 beginning　　**末 end**　　**倒 upside down**
置 arrange

To do something in the wrong or reverse order.
English equivalents: Put the cart before the horse; Topsy-turvy.

不 甘 寂 寞

bù　　gān　　jì　　mò

不甘心被冷落。多指要表现自己，或者参加某一活动。

他们空闲了一段日子后，渐渐不甘寂寞，想找点事情来做。

不 not　　甘 willing　　寂 lonely　　寞 quiet

Someone who has been idle or inactive for some time now wishes to participate in an activity or event.
English equivalents: Make a comeback.

不 言 而 喻

bù yán ér yù

不用解释，就自然明白。

这样的冷淡款待，用意不言而喻，是不想我们来探访你。

不 not　言 told　而 but　喻 understood

To understand something without it being explained.

English equivalents: It goes without saying; Needless to say.

不 自 量 力

bù　　zì　　liàng　　lì

对自己的能力估量过高。

我勉强去做，并非不自量力，而是一心想讨好你。

不 not　自 self　量 measure　力 strength

To overrate one's own ability or physical strength.
English equivalents: Be too cocky/cocksure; Go beyond one's depth.

藏　头　露　尾
cáng　tóu　lù　wěi

形容说话或行动遮遮掩掩，恐怕露出真相。

我看你们一定有什么隐衷，否则不用藏头露尾，害怕被人发现。

藏 hide　头 head　露 expose　尾 tail

Someone trying to cover up something unwittingly reveals his intentions.
English equivalents: Show one's hand.

乘 风 破 浪

chéng　fēng　pò　làng

不畏艰险，奋勇前进。也比喻怀有远大志向。

我单人驾着小船，乘风破浪，想要刷新横渡大西洋的最快记录。

乘 ride　风 wind　破 break　浪 waves

A sailing term used to describe someone forging ahead despite obstacles.
English equivalents: Forge ahead/on; Push ahead/forward.

大 刀 阔 斧

dà　dāo　kuò　fǔ

形容处事果断而有魄力。也比喻做事从大处着眼，爽快而不拘谨。

我办事大刀阔斧，从来不会随便地干。

大 large　　**刀 sword**　　**阔 broad**　　**斧 axe**

(1) To do something resolutely and boldly; or (2) concentrate on large matters without restricting oneself by focusing on minor details.
English equivalents: (1) Go whole hog; (2) Damn the torpedoes, full speed ahead!

大 发 雷 霆
dà   fā   léi   tíng

大发脾气，很忿怒的样子。

今早老板看过他呈交的营业报告后，立刻大发雷霆。

大 greatly   **发 raise**   **雷 thunder**
霆 thunderbolt

Literally, to raise a big burst of thunder. To be angry and shouting.
English equivalents: Come down on someone like a ton of bricks; Explode with rage.

大　惑　不　解

dà　huò　bù　jiě

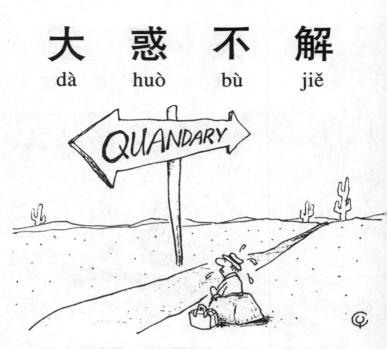

形容十分迷惑，不可理解。

我明明跟着路牌的指示来走，怎么会返回原地，真使我大惑不解!

大 **greatly**　　　惑 **perplexed**　　　不 **not**
解 **understand**

To be thoroughly bewildered.
English equivalents: Be at a loss; Be in a quandary; Beyond one's comprehension.

15

大 失 所 望

dà　shī　suǒ　wàng

希望落空，感觉非常失望。

这个少女，对爱情抱有童话式的幻想，一旦尝试现实生活中的恋爱，就感觉大失所望。

大 great　　失 loss　　所 to　　望 expect

To feel greatly disappointed.
English equivalents: Dash one's hopes; Take the wind out of one's sail.

大　相　径　庭
dà　xiāng　jìng　tíng

形容彼此有很大的差别或矛盾。

他们和我的思想大相径庭；他们重视理论，我则重视实践。

大 great　　　　**相 one another**　　　**径 path**
庭 courtyard

It is some distance from the public path to the courtyard of a private home. Therefore this refers to two distinctly different things or two people with widely divergent opinions.

English equivalents: As different as night and day; Poles apart.

大 有 可 观

dà　　yǒu　　kě　　guān

形容事物美观或内容丰富，很值得一看。

地产经纪极力称赞这座房子大有可观，我却认为它怪里怪气。

今年的艺术节，不但节目多元化，而且请来很多海外艺术家演出，真是大有可观。

大 greatly　有 have　可 suitable　观 viewing

Certain things – a work of art, architecture, literature, the landscape – contain wonders beautiful to see or marvellous to behold.

English equivalents: Beautiful beyond words; A feast for the eyes/mind/senses.

大 智 若 愚

dà　　　zhì　　　ruò　　　yú

才智高的人，会不露锋芒，外表装出愚笨的
样子。

他常常说自己没有什么技能，其实大智若
愚，是一位博学的老师。

大 great　　智 wise　　若 like　　愚 fool

A man of learning does not flaunt his knowledge;
to some he might even appear to be a fool.
English equivalents: Still water runs deep; Hide
one's light under a bushel.

对 症 下 药

duì　　zhèng　　xià　　yào

本指医生针对病症用药。后比喻找出问题的症结所在，才用适当的方法处理。

想根治你的问题，就一定要对症下药。

**对 according to　症 disease　下 prescribe
药 medicine**

To diagnose a disease and prescribe the correct medicine, pinpointing a problem and applying the right remedy.
English equivalent: Put/set something right.

发 号 施 令
fā hào shī lìng

发出命令、指示。

你在外面虽然威风，但回到家里，就不能随便向人发号施令。

发 give　　　　**号 command**　　　　**施 execute**
令 order

To order people about.
English equivalents: Boss someone around; Lord it over someone.

发　人　深　省
fā　rén　shēn　xǐng

启发人去深思和反省。

我喜欢莎士比亚的作品，因为当中有很多发人深省的说话。

发 induce　　　**人 person**　　　**深 deep**
省 reflection

A word, act or deed which provokes deep thought about something.
English equivalents: Provide food for thought; Set one to think.

风　驰　电　掣
fēng　chí　diàn　chè

形容行动非常迅速

风大雨大，不要风驰电掣，还是小心慢驶吧！

风 wind　驰 dash　电 lightning　掣 flash

Things or people moving fast are often said to go like the wind and have the speed of lightning. That's exactly what this expression says.
English equivalents: As fast/ swift as lightning; Quick as a flash.

风 风 雨 雨

fēng   fēng   yǔ   yǔ

刮风下雨。比喻重重障碍。也指议论纷纷。

我在这公司工作了十多年，经过几许风风雨雨，现在发生的，不过是小小的风波。

风 wind   **风wind**   **雨 rain**   **雨 rain**

The wind and rain in this idiom represent (1) troubles and hardships over a period of time; or (2) widespread controversy over something.
English equivalents: (1) Trials and tribulations; (2) A storm of controversy.

改 邪 归 正
gǎi　xié　guī　zhèng

改正坏的行为，做个好人。

他的本性善良，我相信能够感化他，使他改邪归正。

改 give up　邪 evil　归 return　正 good

This is a message for those who have gone astray: give up one's wicked ways and return to a life of righteousness.
English equivalents: Mend one's way; Turn over a new leaf.

各 奔 前 程

gè　　bèn　　qián　　chéng

彼此志向不同，各自为前途打算。

我们追求的目标不同，只有各奔前程，才能
发挥抱负。

**各 each　奔 go　前 ahead　程 (own) way
前程 the future.**

Each going his own way in pursuit of his destiny.
English equivalents: Strike out on one's own.

各　式　各　样

gè　　shì　　gè　　yàng

不同的式样及种类。

我们的小镇虽小，但有各式各样的建筑物，既新奇又富想象力。

各 every　式 shape　各 every　样 kind

All sorts of people, style, architecture, fashion, etc.

English equivalents: Of every description; It/They come(s) in all shapes and sizes.

27

根　深　蒂　固

gēn　shēn　dì　gù

根基很牢固，不易动摇。

这个问题根深蒂固，恐怕我们要花很长时间，才能解决。

根 roots　深 deep　蒂 stalks　固 sturdy

The roots and stalks here are traits, habits or problems deeply ingrained in a person, a business, society, etc. They could be anything from an established mannerism to a cultural tradition.
English equivalents: Deep-rooted; Deep-seated.

勾 心 斗 角
gōu　xīn　dòu　jiǎo

各用心机，互相排斥。

想伤害我们的敌人已经太多，还是不要勾心斗角，同类相残。

勾 hook　心 heart　斗 struggle　角 horn

Though this expression referred originally to the architectural complexities of a royal palace, it now describes people scheming to outdo one another. ***English equivalents:*** Get the better of someone; Jockey for position.

孤　陌　寡　闻
gū　　lòu　　guǎ　　wén

形容学识浅薄，见闻不广。

我见的世面不多，孤陋寡闻，怎能提供什么意见呢!

孤 isolated　　　　**陋 ignorant**　　　　**寡 little**
闻 awareness

To have scanty knowledge of something or be ill-informed.
English equivalents: Not know the time of day;
Not know chalk from cheese.

孤　掌　难　鸣
gū　　zhǎng　　nán　　míng

IF WE GET TOGETHER WE CAN MAKE A RACKET!

个人的力量单薄，难有作为。

你是我的好帮手，没有你，我孤掌难鸣。

孤 single　掌 palm　难 difficult　鸣 sound

One palm cannot clap. In the same way, one cannot do much without the support and co-operation of others.

English equivalents: No man is an island unto itself.

光　明　正　大
guāng　　míng　　zhèng　　dà

心地坦白，正直无私。

我为人光明正大，从来不做蒙骗他人的事情。

光 light　明 bright　正 upright　大 great

This describes someone fair, honest and upright.
English equivalents: Be fair and square; Honest as the day is long.

鬼 鬼 崇 崇
guǐ guǐ suì suì

形容行动诡秘，恐怕别人发现。

你在里面鬼鬼祟祟的，是否干着见不得人的事情。

鬼 ghost   **鬼 ghost**   **祟 evil spirit**
祟 evil spirit

To sneak around suspiciously.
English equivalents: Up to hanky-panky; Up to no good.

过 犹 不 及
guò　yóu　bù　jí

做事做过了头，就跟做得不够一样，都是不好的。

他不过犯了小错，却被你严厉惩罚，真是过犹不及！

过 **excess**　犹 **like**　不 **not**　及 **enough**

Too much of something is as bad as not having enough of it. Doing too much is as bad as not doing enough.
English equivalents: Go overboard.

何 去 何 从
hé qù hé cóng

感觉彷徨、无主见。

在这个陌生的地方，他把钱花得精光，还找不着表亲，一时间不知何去何从。

何 where　去 go　何 where　从 follow

To be confused about where to go, what to do or how to act.

English equivalents: At a loss; Not know whether one is coming or going.

画 蛇 添 足
huà　shé　tiān　zú

做多余的事，有害无益，反而坏了事情。

原本标致的一个设计，给你画蛇添足，变得很滑稽。

画 draw　　蛇 snake　　添 add　　足 feet

To spoil the effect by doing something superfluous.

English equivalents: Gild the lily; Too much of a good thing.

急　不　可　待
jí　bù　kě　dài

心情急切，不能等待。

想到快要和家人团聚，他们急不可待，嚷着立刻起程。

急 impatient　不 not　可 able　待 wait

Too impatient to wait.
English equivalents: Have ants in one's pants;
Champ/Chafe/Strain at the bit.

机 不 可 失

jī　　bù　　kě　　shī

时机难得，不可错失。

这是个大好机会，千万机不可失，要好好把握。

机 opportunity　　不 not　　可 can　　失 lose

Do not let a good opportunity slip by.
English equivalents: A window of opportunity;
(U.S) Go for it; Now or never; Opportunity only
knocks once.

疾 言 厉 色
jí yán lì sè

形容发怒时，说话急迫，面色严厉。

被他疾言厉色地骂过，我以后也不敢偷摘他的果实。

疾 harsh   **言 word**   **厉 grave**
色 expression

To reprimand sternly and profusely.
English equivalents: Blow one's top; Have/Throw a conniption fit; Vent one's anger/rage.

家 喻 户 晓

jiā   yù   hù   xiǎo

家家户户都知道。

这个小镇只有十多户人家，不论发生大小事情，很快就家喻户晓。

家 family   **喻 understand**   **户 household**
晓 know

Known to every household.
English equivalents: Be the talk of the town; Be a household name/word.

贱 如 粪 土

jiàn   rú   fèn   tǔ

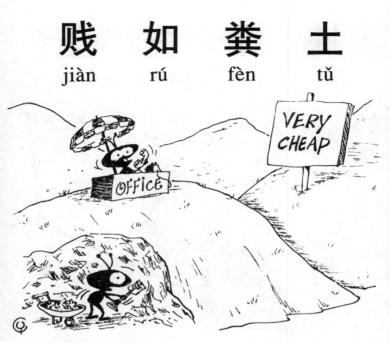

形容毫无价值。

他是个非常出色的推销员，就算贱如粪土的
东西，也有办法销售。

贱 cheap   如 as   粪 manure   土 soil

Describes things considered to be of little or no
value.
English equivalents: As cheap as dirt; Not worth
a damn/a hill of beans/a rap.

捷 足 先 登

jié　　　zú　　　xiān　　　dēng

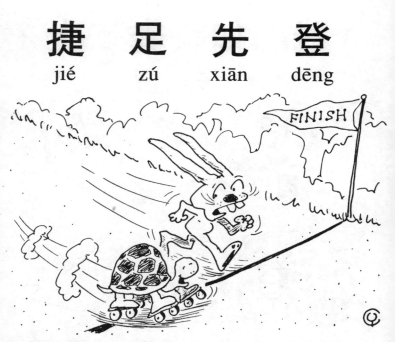

因行动较快而先达到目的。

这是一个竞争激烈的社会，稍一松懈，就给别人捷足先登。

捷 swift　　足 foot　　先 first　　登 arrive

The one who is the first to act achieves success.
English equivalents: The early bird catches the worm; First come, first served.

荆 棘 载 途

jīng　　　jí　　　zài　　　tú

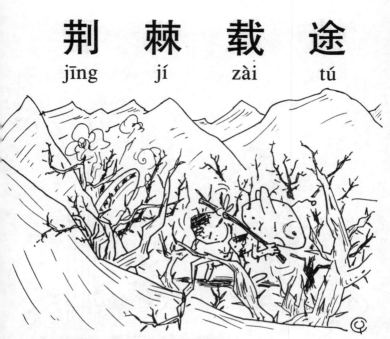

比喻情况艰难，障碍重重。

这次的探险旅程是荆棘载途；首先机件失灵，跟着迷失方向，差点儿连生命也送掉。

荆 thorny plant　　　　　棘 thorny plant
载 all over　　　　途 path

Describes encountering many obstacles and pitfalls while doing something.
English equivalents: Have a hard time; Trials and tribulations.

慷 慨 解 囊
kāng kǎi jiě náng

毫不吝啬的用钱帮助别人。

虽然外婆很节俭，可是十分热心公益，经常慷慨解囊。

慷 fervently   **慨** generous   **解** undo
囊 purse
慷慨 generous

To give money generously to help somebody.
English equivalents: Dip/Put one's hand in one's pocket/purse; Loosen/Open the purse strings.

苦 尽 甘 来
kǔ jìn gān lái

艰苦的日子已过去，幸福的日子将来临。

你只要忍耐一点，我保证一定苦尽甘来，再过甜蜜的生活。

苦 bitterness　　　**尽 end**　　**甘 sweetness**
来 come

Happiness begins when suffering or unhappiness ends.
English equivalents: A change for the better; Fair weather follows the rain.

令 人 发 指
lìng　　rén　　fà　　zhǐ

使人愤怒到极点。

他做错事，还要向人发脾气，真是令人发指。

令 **make** 人 **person** 发 **hair** 指 **stand up**

To make someone very angry.
English equivalents: Ruffle someone's feathers;
Set someone's teeth on edge.

路 不 拾 遗
lù　bù　shí　yí

路有失物，不拾取当为己有。比喻人诚实而不贪心。

我虽然穷，但谨守路不拾遗的美德，不会贪图失物。

路 road　　　　**不 not**　　　　**拾 pick up**
遗 lost object

Describes an honest person who does not pick up or pocket things not belonging to him; also describes a society with a high moral standard in which honesty prevails.

满 载 而 归

mǎn zài ér guī

得了很大收获回来.

他每次旅游回来，都满载而归，大包小包的塞满了旅行袋。

满 **fully**　　　载 **loaded**　　　而 **then**
归 **return(home)**

To return home — from the market, from travelling, from a business mission, etc — fully loaded with things or fruitful results. Even a thief could use this after a successful foray!

English equivalents: Have a good catch; Make a haul.

忙 中 有 错

máng　　zhōng　　yǒu　　cuò

太过繁忙时，难免做错。

你每天办的事情很多，偶然忙中有错，也不必过份怪责自己。

忙 **hurry**　中 **within**　有 **have**　错 **mistake**

One is likely to make mistakes when one is in a hurry.

English equivalents: Haste makes waste; (Humorous) The hurrieder I go, the behinder I get.

美 中 不 足

měi　　zhōng　　bù　　zú

大体上很美好，可惜有些少缺憾。

这面镜子很精致，可是美中不足，镜框有一点破损。

**美 beauty　中 within　不 not　足 sufficient
不足 inadequacy**

A blemish in an otherwise perfect or beautiful thing.
English equivalent: A fly in the ointment.

面　目　全　非
miàn　mù　quán　fēi

形容完全改变，跟原先的模样不同。

从前这里有一座华美的大房子，现在面目全非，只剩下一片瓦砾。

面 face　　　**目 eye**　　　**全 completely**
非 different
面目 appearance

The appearance of something has been completely changed.
English equivalents: Changed beyond all recognition; Put on a different look.

目　空　一　切
mù　kōng　yī　qiè

什么都不看在眼里。比喻人狂妄，非常自负。

这个人目空一切，从来想做就做，不理会别人的反应。

**目 behold　空 nothing　一 one　切 all
一切 everything**

Describes someone who thinks highly of himself and views everyone with a scornful eye.
English equivalents: Have one's nose in the air; Be high and mighty.

能　屈　能　伸
néng　qū　néng　shēn

比喻顺应环境，失意时屈就，得意时施展抱负。

我处事能屈能伸，加上懂得变通，不难替自己制造有利发展的机会。

能 able　屈 bend　能 able　伸 stretch

Be able to endure humiliation in an adverse situation and stay resilient at all times.
English equivalents: Bear through/up; Bide one's time.

怒 火 中 烧
nù　huǒ　zhōng　shāo

形容非常愤怒。

他在小小的后园举火烧烤，差点把邻居的房屋烧毁，难怪他们怒火中烧。

怒 angry　火 fire　中 inside　烧 burning

To be exceedingly angry.
English equivalents: Blow one's top; Red with rage; Hot and bothered; Hot under the collar.

气　急　败　坏

qì　　jí　　bài　　huài

指上气不接下气，非常慌张的样子。

你知道我遇上困难，就气急败坏的赶来看我，使我十分感动。

气 breathing　　急 fast　　败 shatter
坏 devastate

This idiom describes someone so anxious and unnerved that he is virtually gasping for air.
English equivalents: Have a (bad) case of the jitters; In a state of shock.

杞 人 忧 天

qǐ   rén   yōu   tiān

形容过分忧虑。

他最爱杞人忧天，事情还未发生，已经作最坏的打算。

杞 Qi   **人 person**   **忧 worry**   **天 sky**

Someone in the ancient kingdom of Qi worried the sky might collapse. This describes someone who worries unnecessarily.
English equivalents: A Chicken Little; Be a worrywart.

前 功 尽 弃
qián   gōng   jìn   qì

事情将要成功却忽然失败，使所有努力白费。

我爬上了山峰，以为到达终点，岂料发现走错了路，结果前功尽弃。

前 previous   功 effort   尽 all   弃 wasted

Something happens on the verge of success and spoils all that has been achieved.
English equivalents: A washout; All in vain; Go down the drain.

倾 家 荡 产
qīng jiā dàng chǎn

用尽全部家产。

他继承父亲的生意后，因为不善经营，弄到倾家荡产。

倾 collapse　　　**家 family**　　　**荡 wipe out**
产 property

To be reduced to poverty by losing or squandering the family fortune.
English equivalents: Go to rack and ruin; Go to the dogs.

穷 思 极 想

qióng　　sī　　jí　　xiǎng

用尽心力去思索。

这座石像是他心血结晶，替它题名，就穷思
极想了好几天。

**穷 exhaustively　　思 think　　极 thoroughly
想 ponder**

To think exhaustively about something.
English equivalents: Rack one's brain; Turn
something over in one's mind.

人 穷 志 短

rén　　qióng　　zhì　　duǎn

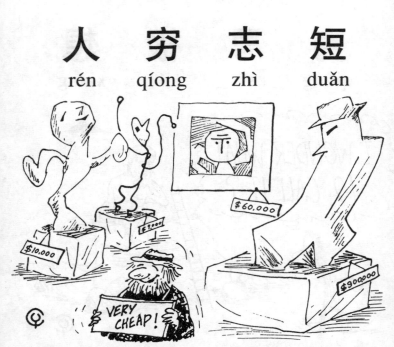

形容人处境艰难窘迫，意气消沉，变得没有大志。

我虽然要为生活奔波，但不会人穷志短，和你们合作骗人的勾当。

**人 person　　　　穷 poor　　　　志 ambition
短 lacking**

A poor person lacks ambition.

人　微　言　轻
rén　　wēi　　yán　　qīng

地位低微，说话不受重视。

他不过是公司里的小职员，人微言轻，当然
没有人考虑他的提议。

人 person　微 lowly　言 word　轻 slight

A lowly person's opinions carry little weight.

日 复 一 日
rì　fù　yī　rì

过了一天又一天。

这里的工作刻板，日复一日，渐渐地我有点厌倦了。

日 day　复 repeat　一 one　日 day

As one day comes to an end, another follows.
English equivalents: Day after day; Day in day out; From day to day.

日 上 三 竿
rì　shàng　sān　gān

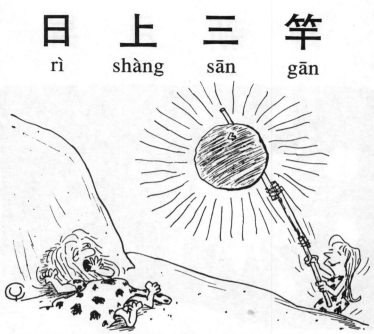

太阳升上三根竹竿的高度，约早上八九时。
比喻时候不早。

昨天我工作至深夜三时，所以今天睡至日上三竿。

日 sun　上 ascends　三 three　竿 rods

The sun has risen to the height of three bamboo
rods, it is late in the morning. This idiom taunts
someone who is late getting out of bed.
English equivalent: A ten o'clock scholar.

日　新　月　异
rì　xīn　yuè　yì

每天都有新奇的东西出现，表示事物发展迅速。

世间的事物日新月异，常常学习，才不怕与时代脱节。

日 day　　新 new　　月 month　　异 different

Things are in constant change: new ideas and inventions are continually appearing.
English equivalents: There is always something new under the sun.

如 愿 以 偿
rú　yuàn　yǐ　cháng

愿望得到实现。

她说："我的梦中情人是一位英俊、智慧、显贵……的王子。"

我微笑着答："想如愿以偿，就要看妳的运气！"

如 as　愿 wished　以 already　偿 fulfilled

Have one's wish fulfilled.
English equivalents: An/The answer to one's prayers; A dream come true.

身 不 由 主

shēn   bù   yóu   zhǔ

失去自由，完全受他人支配。

时势发展到现在的地步，我变得身不由主，被人束缚。

身 body   **不 not**   **由 obey**   **主 oneself**

To be under someone's control.
English equivalents: Held in check; Led by the nose; Not one's own master.

视　死　如　归
shì　sǐ　rú　guī

把死亡看作归家一样。比喻人不怕死。

如果一个人抱着视死如归的精神，就什么都敢去做。

视 view　死 death　如 as　归 return (home)

To face death calmly and without fear.
English equivalents: At peace with one's maker.

手　到　擒　来
shǒu　　dào　　qín　　lái

一伸手就捉着敌人。比喻易做，不费气力。

我掌握了他所有的罪证，要获得胜诉，已经手到擒来。

手 hand　　　　**到 reach**　　　**擒 catch**
来 from there to here

Accomplish something effortlessly.
English equivalents: Be a breeze; As easy/
simple as falling off a log.

守 口 如 瓶

shǒu　　kǒu　　rú　　píng

说话谨慎或严守秘密。

你心里面有什么不高兴的事，不妨尽情倾
诉，我们保证守口如瓶。

守 keep　　口 mouth　　如 like　　瓶 jar

To be absolutely silent; to keep a secret.
English equivalents: Keep one's mouth closed/
shut; Keep the lid on something.

守　望　相　助
shǒu　　wàng　　xiāng　　zhù

邻居之间，互相照顾和共同防守附近的治安。

街坊会成立后，邻居们守望相助，立刻改善了这一区的保安情况。

守 keep　望 watch　相 one another　助 help

To keep watch against crime and give mutual help in a neighbourhood.
English equivalent: Give/Lend a helping hand.

蜀 犬 吠 日

shǔ　quǎn　fèi　rì

比喻见识少，对平常事情也觉得惊奇。

这不是稀奇的事情，只要你多些出门见识，就不会蜀犬吠日。

蜀 Sichuan　犬 dog　吠 bark at　日 sun

The sun is a stranger in the foggy province of Sichuan, hence this idiom that describes an unworldly person who expresses surprise at ordinary things.

English equivalents: Make a fuss over nothing/ trifles; Much ado about nothing.

顺 手 牵 羊
shùn　shǒu　qiān　yáng

比喻随手取去他人的东西。

发觉心爱的宠物给人顺手牵羊，他伤心到整夜睡不着。

**顺 conveniently　手 hand　牵 lead away
羊 sheep**

To steal something, especially when it is easy to do – like stealing a sheep from someone's pasture. *English equivalents:* Like taking candy from a baby; Walk off with something.

似 是 而 非

sì   shì   ér   fēi

好象对，其实不对。

你提出的理论，似是而非，很难说服我。

似 seems   是 right   而 but   非 wrong

Something is not what it seems to be.
English equivalent: Not what it's cracked up/
made out to be.

同 病 相 怜

tóng　　bìng　　xiāng　　lián

遭遇同样不幸的人，自然互相同情。

他们同病相怜，了解彼此的感受，所以谈得很投契。

同 same　　病 ailment　　相 one another
怜 sympathize

Those with the same misfortune show sympathy and understanding for one another.
English equivalents: In the same boat; In tune with someone.

同 流 合 污

tóng　　liú　　hé　　wū

跟坏人为伍，一起做坏事。

你和不良份子交往，迟早受影响，跟他们同流合污。

同 **same**　流 **stream**　合 **jointly**　污 **dirty**

To collaborate with someone in an evil venture.
English equivalent: Partners in crime.

头 头 是 道

tóu　　tóu　　shì　　dào

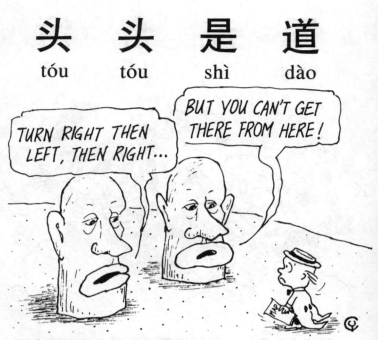

形容说话做事有条有理。

你们提出的意见不同，但都分析得头头是道，我听从谁人好呢!

头 direction　　头 direction　　是 be　　道 road

To speak or do things in an orderly and logical way.
English equivalents: Be well-ordered; Show good sense.

徒 劳 无 功
tú　láo　wú　gōng

白费气力，却没有获得一点利益或成就。

他没有研究过这里的土质，就胡乱种植，结果徒劳无功，没有收成。

徒 waste　　**劳 effort**　　**无 without**
功 achievement

To work and strive for something without success.
English equivalents: Go on a wild goose chase; Labour in vain.

万　无　一　失

wàn　　wú　　yī　　shī

十分有把握，不会出错。

我的计划十分周详，保证万无一失。

万 ten thousand　　**无 without**　　**一 single**
失 failure

Describes a strategy or a measure which is very safe or certain of success.
English equivalents: A sure thing; Safe and sound; Sure fire.

忘 恩 负 义
wàng　　ēn　　fù　　yì

不但忘记别人的恩义，而且做出对不起别人
的事。

我供你吃、供你住，现在竟然忘恩负义，把
我欺负。

忘 forget 恩 favour 负 contradict 义 virtue

To ignore what someone has done to help you.
Be ungrateful.
English equivalents: Bite the hand that feeds
you.

亡 羊 补 牢
wáng yáng bǔ láo

比喻事后补救。

当大部分的员工离开后，他才懂得亡羊补牢，改善工作环境。

亡 lose　　羊 sheep　　补 mend　　牢 pen

Even after a mistake it is not too late to correct things.
English equivalents: Better late than never; Close/Lock the stable door after the horse has bolted.

尾 随 不 舍

wěi　　súi　　bù　　shě

紧紧的跟随着，毫不放松。

你以为摆脱了我，岂料我尾随不舍，一直跟踪而来。

尾 back　　随 follow　　不 not　　舍 give up

To follow closely behind someone.
English equivalents: Dog/Tail someone; In hot pursuit.

问 道 于 盲

wèn　　dào　　yú　　máng

比喻向无知识的人求教。

我不认识这里的地理环境，向我问路，等于
问道于盲。

问 ask　　**道 way**　　**于 from**　　**盲 blind**

To seek advice from someone ill-informed on the
subject.
English equivalent: The blind leading the blind.

我 行 我 素

wǒ   xíng   wǒ   sù

完全按照自己意愿行动，绝对不受他人或环境影响。

他从来做事我行我素，不喜欢请教别人意见。

我 I   行 act   我 my   素 usual way

To act completely according to one's wishes without bothering what others say.
English equivalents: To be a law unto oneself; Take one's own course.

五 彩 缤 纷
wǔ　cǎi　bīn　fēn

形容颜色繁多，光彩悦目。

他设计的头饰很美丽，五彩缤纷，可以配衬不同颜色的衣裳。

五 five　彩 colours　缤 opulent　纷 jumbled

Descriptive of something very colourful.
English equivalents: Awashed/Blazoned with colour; A blaze/riot of colour.

无　法　无　天
wú　　fǎ　　wú　　tiān

形容横行无忌，完全不遵守纪律或法则。

这是一个什么的社会，无法无天的匪徒，连天真的小孩子都欺负。

无 no　　　法 law　　　无 no　　　天 heaven

To act with total disregard for the law.
English equivalents: A breakdown in law and order; Run wild

无　微　不　至

wú　　wēi　　bù　　zhì

形容很关怀和照顾得十分细心、周到。

这间酒店的服务员，招待顾客无微不至，使人感觉亲切舒服。

无 no　　　　**微 minute detail**　　　　**不 not**
至 attended

To attend to something or take care of someone meticulously.
English equivalents: Show every concern; Take great pains; Wait on someone hand and foot.

无 心 之 过

wú　xīn　zhī　guò

不是故意犯的过错。

我不是存心破坏你的计划，这是无心之过，
请你原谅我吧!

无 without　心 heart　之 of　过 mistake

To make a mistake unwittingly.
English equivalents: A goof-up.

想　入　非　非
xiǎng　rù　fēi　fēi

形容想象奇怪，不切实际。

我的小侄儿很天真，在乡间拾了一只蛋，就想入非非，问我它会不会孵出一只大恐龙。

想 think　入 into　非 fantasy　非 fantasy

To indulge in fantasy.
English equivalents: Let one's imagination run wild; Have pipe dreams.

小　题　大　作
xiǎo　tí　dà　zuò

把小事夸大，当大事处理。

这不过是小小毛病，也要请专家解决，真是小题大作!

小 small　题 matter　大 big　作 do

Make a big issue out of a small matter.
English equivalents: Big deal; Make a mountain out of a molehill.

小　心　翼　翼
xiǎo　xīn　yì　yì

非常谨慎，不敢稍有疏忽。

这是个新尝试，难怪她小心心翼翼地进行。

小 little　心 heart　翼 cautious　翼 cautious
小心 careful

To do something very carefully.
English equivalents: Easy does it; With the greatest care.

心　花　怒　放

xīn　huā　nù　fàng

心里高兴得象花朵盛开，比喻非常快乐。

看见亲手栽培的幼苗长大，还开出灿烂的花朵，他不禁心花怒放。

心 heart　花 flower　怒 full　放 bloom

A beautiful and poetic way of describing being very, very happy.

English equivalents: As happy as a lark; One's heart sings with joy.

心　力　交　瘁
xīn　lì　jiāo　cuì

精神和体力都用尽。指极度劳累。

他办事认真，不论大小工作，都做到心力交瘁。

心 heart　　　　**力 strength**　　　　**交 both**
瘁 exhausted

To be totally exhausted mentally and physically.
English equivalents: Dead/Dog tired; Played out;
Worn out.

欣 欣 向 荣

xīn　　xīn　　xiàng　　róng

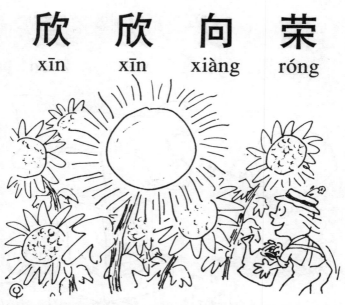

形容草木生长茂盛。也指事业兴旺发达。

看见一田园的太阳花欣欣向荣，在阳光下闪耀着金黄的颜色的，我心里好不高兴。

他努力经营的花店欣欣向荣，两年间，已开设了五间分店。

**欣 joyously　　欣 joyously　　向 towards
荣 prosperity**

Describes the state of a thriving plant or a business.
English equivalents: In full bloom; Doing a roaring business.

信 以 为 真

xìn　　yǐ　　wéi　　zhēn

不辨真伪，就相信了。

他思想单纯，别人的说话，常常信以为真。

信 believe　以 make　为 as　真 authentic

To believe or accept something as true.
English equivalents: Take/Accept something at
face value; Take one's word for it.

形　销　骨　立
xíng　xiāo　gǔ　lì

形容身体十分消瘦。

她离开后，他不愿吃，也不愿休息，弄到形
销骨立。

形 **body**　　销 **waste away**　　骨 **bone**
立 **stand out**

To become very thin.
English equivalents: A bag of bones; As thin as
a rake; Just skin and bones.

眼 明 手 快
yǎn　míng　shǒu　kuài

目光锐利，办事敏捷。

他眼明手快，早已把事情做妥，不用担心呢!

眼 eye　明 sharp　手 hand　快 nimble

To be efficient, quick to react, and able to complete a task without delay.
English equivalents: On the ball; Quick off the mark; Quick on the uptake.

亦 步 亦 趋

yì　　bù　　yì　　qū

本指学生向老师学习。比喻模仿别人。

很多少年人深受偶像影响，对他们的衣着举动，亦步亦趋。

亦 also　　步 step　　亦 also　　趋 follow

To copy someone or something closely in behaviour, fashion, design, speech, etc.
English equivalents: To ape/mirror/parrot/someone; Follow in someone's wake.

异 口 同 声

yì　　kǒu　　tóng　　shēng

指众人意见一致。

这个小岛的居民大部分异口同声，反对把它发展为旅游区，恐怕一向恬静的生活受到干扰。

异 different　口 mouths　同 same　声 voice

To speak or agree in unison.
English equivalents: To have the same opinion about something; to speak or agree in unison.

以 卵 击 石

yǐ   luǎn   jī   shí

比喻以弱敌强，必定失败。

他很强壮，和他硬碰是以卵击石，还是运用计谋取胜吧!

以 use   卵 egg   击 hit   石 stone

A metaphor for someone weak fighting against a strong enemy.
English equivalents: To fight a losing battle; Hit one's head against a stone wall.

一 落 千 丈

yī　　luò　　qiān　　zhàng

形容境况、地位、声誉等急剧下降。

父母的关系恶化后，他不再专心读书，成绩一落千丈。

一 **one**　　落 **fall**　　千 **thousand**　　丈 **ten feet**

A rapid decline in one's performance, fortune, business, etc.

English equivalents: Go to pot; Go to rack and ruin.

一 目 了 然

yī　　mù　　liǎo　　rán

看一眼，就完全明白。

这种望远镜的结构简单，一目了然，很容易操作。

一 one　　　　**目 glance**　　　　**了 understand**
然 -ing(suffix)

To understand everything at a glance.
English equivalents: As plain as the nose on one's face; Catch on; Get the idea/picture.

一 诺 千 金
yī　nuò　qiān　jīn

比喻诺言诚实可靠。

我从来一诺千金，答应你们的事，一定会办妥。

一 one　诺 promise　千 thousand　金 gold

Describes someone whose promise can be trusted.

English equivalents: As good as one's word; One's word is golden.

一 无 所 得

yī　　wú　　suǒ　　dé

什么也没有得到。

我天天照顾你们，但你们有没有关心过我，
难道我的劳苦是一无所得？

一 one (thing)　无 without　所 to　得 gain

Someone does something yet reaps no reward
nor wins praise for his efforts.
English equivalents: Be of no avail; A waste of
time and effort.

意　想　不　到
yì　　xiǎng　　bù　　dào

没有料想到。

他为人乐观，竟然会独自躲在一旁不开心，
令人意想不到。

意 anticipate　想 think　不 not　到 reach

Something happens that has not been anticipated.
English equivalents: From out of nowhere/the
blue; It comes as a complete/utter surprise.

一　叶　知　秋

yī　　yè　　zhī　　qiū

比喻从小迹象，可推测事态的发展趋势。

从人们忽然节约衣服、饮食和娱乐的开支，可以一叶知秋，感觉社会经济已走下坡。

一 one　　叶 leaf　　知 know　　秋 autumn

The observation of a small sign can reveal the general trend of development of something or a situation.

English equivalents: Little things mean a lot; A straw in the wind.

一 针 见 血

yī　　zhēn　　jiàn　　xiě

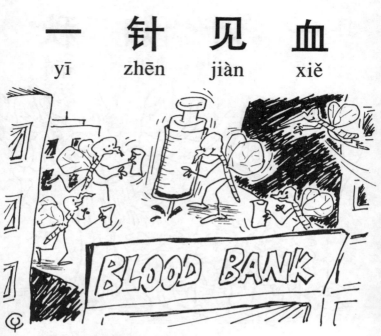

比喻言辞直接而中肯。

他的提议一针见血，使我们忽然明白怎样处理这个困难。

一 **one**　针 **prick**　见 **see**　血 **blood**

Descriptive of someone's speech or writing style which goes directly to the central point.
English equivalents: Hit the nail on the head; Right/Straight to the point.

一 知 半 解

yī　　zhī　　bàn　　jiě

知道得不全面，似懂非懂。

你们既然对这个问题一知半解，怎么不向老师发问呢？

一 **one**　知 **know**　半 **half**　解 **comprehend**

To have a little or a superficial knowledge about something.
English equivalents: Know ever so little/next to nothing about something; Know about it after a fashion.

一 掷 千 金

yī zhì qīan jīn

原指赌徒用千金投注。比喻滥用金钱，不知节制。

他爱搜购珍奇雀鸟，为了得到罕有的品种，常常不惜一掷千金。

一 **one** 掷 **fling** 千 **thousand** 金 **gold**

This originally referred to gamblers who made huge bets. Today, it refers to someone who spends lavishly and wastefully.

English equivalents: A big/high spender; Spend money like water.

引　人　入　胜

yǐn　　rén　　rù　　shèng

形容文字、言论或景色由平淡渐入佳境，使人十分喜爱和投入。

这里的风景引人入胜，使人乐而忘返。

他讲的故事引人入胜，老人家和小孩子都喜欢听，

引 attract　　人 person　　入 into
胜 enchantment

Describes a story or a sight so fascinating that it completely captivates the listener or viewer.
English equivalents: A transport of delights; Go/Fall into raptures.

应　有　尽　有
yīng　yǒu　jìn　yǒu

应有的都有，指一切齐备。

本店规模虽小，但货色齐全，应有尽有。

应 should　　有 have　　尽 all　　有 have

A place that is well-equipped and has everything one expects to find.

English equivalents: From A to Z; From soup to nuts.

勇 往 直 前
yǒng wǎng zhí qián

毫不畏惧，奋勇地一直前进。

一路上，他们虽然遇到不少的障碍，但勇往直前，终於抵达目的地。

勇 bravely 往 go 直 straight 前 ahead

To forge ahead undeterred by obstacles.
English equivalents: To forge ahead; Show true grit.

犹 豫 不 决
yóu yù bù jué

犹疑，不能立定主意。

他既然给你发挥机会，那么不要犹豫不决，立刻行动吧!

犹 still 豫 hesitant 不 not 决 decided

Unable to make up one's mind.
English equivalents: To dilly-dally; To hem and haw about.

与 日 俱 增
yǔ　rì　jù　zēng

比喻不断地增长，或者增长得很快。

经你悉心教导后，小儿对数学的兴趣与日俱增。

与 with　日 day　俱 together　增 increase

Increasing day by day. It can be knowledge, business, technology, one's interest, feelings, etc.
English equivalents: Making strides; On the rise/upgrade.

趾 高 气 扬
zhǐ　　gāo　　qì　　yáng

装出神气十足，很了不起的样子。

他升职后，变得趾高气扬，不再和小职员来往。

趾 toe　　高 high　　气 airs　　扬 display

Describes someone who is very proud and arrogant.

English equivalents: Give oneself airs; Have one's nose in the air; Put on airs and graces.

执　迷　不　悟

zhí　　mí　　bù　　wù

固执入迷，不知觉悟。

你既然知道走错了路，怎么还执迷不悟？

执 persist　　　**迷 bewilderment**　　　**不 not**
悟 awaken

To persist in a wrong course and refuse to learn the truth.
English equivalents: Close/Shut one's ears/eyes to something; Refuse to come to one's senses.

志 同 道 合
zhì　　tóng　　dào　　hé

彼此的志趣、理想都相同。

他们志同道合，计划一起做点小生意。

志 ideals　同 same　道 path　合 agreeable

To have and cherish the same ideals and interests.
English equivalents: Birds of a feather flock together.

置 之 不 理

zhī　　zhì　　bù　　lǐ

弃置一旁，不加理会。

这是一个紧急要求，我绝对不能置之不理，
而且要立刻解决。

置 put aside　之 it　不 not　理 attend

To disregard something.
English equivalents: Close one's eyes to something; Sweep something under the carpet.

罪 魁 祸 首
zuì　kuí　huò　shǒu

带领别人作恶犯罪的人。

不要看他一副嬉皮笑脸的样子，其实是陷害
我们的罪魁祸首。

罪 crime　魁 chief　祸 disaster　首 leader

The main culprit.
English equivalents: Godfather; Criminal chieftain;
Underworld kingpin.

坐 井 观 天
zuò　jǐng　guān　tiān

比喻见识狭小浅薄。

要扩大视野，就不能常常呆在家里坐井观天。

坐 sit (in)　井 well　观 observe　天 sky

To have a narrow view as a result of under-exposure to the world.
English equivalents: Be narrow-minded; Not see beyond one's nose.

作 威 作 福
zuò wēi zuò fú

滥用权势，欺压他人。

他恃着父亲是校董，小小年纪就作威作福，欺侮同学。

作 act   威 powerful   作 act   福 favoured

To bully people by abusing one's power.
English equivalents: Ride roughshod over others; Lord it over someone; Throw one's weight around.

坐 享 其 成

zuò　　xiǎng　　qí　　chéng

没有出力，却享用他人努力得来的成果。

别人辛辛苦苦地工作时，你就躲在一旁，现在却坐享其成。

坐 sit　享 enjoy　其 another's　成 success

To enjoy the rewards of success that rightfully belong to someone else.
English equivalents: Get someting for nothing; Live in the light of someone's glory.

English Equivalents

A bag of bones 95
A big/high spender 108
A blaze/riot of colour 84
A break down in law and order 85
A change for the better 45
A Chicken Little 56
A dream come true 65
A feast for the eyes/mind/senses 18
A fly in the ointment 50
A God-father 118
A goof-up 87
A Scrooge 3
A stab in the back 6
A storm of controversy 24
A straw in the wind 105
A sure thing 78
A ten o' clock scholar 63
A transport of delights 109
A washout 57
A waste of time and effort 103
A window of opportunity 38
All in vain 57
An/The answer to one's prayers 65
As cheap as dirt 41
As different as night and day 17
As easy as falling off a log 68
As fast/swift as lightning 23
As good as one's word 102
As happy as a lark 91
As plain as a pikestaff 101
As plain as one's nose on one's face 101
As thin as a rake 95
At a lost 15, 35
At peace with one's maker 67
Awashed/Blazoned with colour 84
Be a breeze 68
Be a household name 40
Be a money-grubber 3
Be a washout 100
Be a worrywart 56
Be fair and square 32
Be high and mighty 52
Be in a quandary 15
Be narrow minded 119
Be of no avail 103
Be of one mind/voice 98

Be the talk of the town 40
Be well-ordered 76
Bear through/up 53
Beautiful beyond words 18
Better late than never 80
Beyond one's comprehension 15
Bide one's time 53
Big deal 89
Birds of a feather flock together 116
Bite the hand that feeds you 79
Blow one's top 39, 54
Boss someone around 21
Champ/Chafe/Strain at the bit 37
Changed beyond all recognition 51
Close/Shut one's ears/eyes to something 115, 117
Close/Lock the stable door after the horse has bolted 80
Come down on someone like a ton of bricks 14
Criminal chieftain 118
Damn the torpedoes, fuel speed ahead 13
Dash one's hopes 16
Day after day 62
Day in day out 62
Dead/Dog tired 92
Deep-rooted 28
Deep-seated 28
Dip/Put one's hand into one's pocket/purse 44
Dog/Tail someone 81
Doing a roaring business 93
Easy does it 90
Explode with rage 14
Fair weather follows the rain 45
Fight to the bitter end 4
First come, first served 41
Follow in someone's wake 97
Forge ahead/on 12
From A to Z 110
From day to day 62
From out of nowhere/the blue 104
From soup to nuts 110
Get the better of someone 29
Get the idea/picture 101
Gild the lily 36

125